Making the Case for Socialism

An Examination of the
Accomplishments of Socialism

James R. King

8/09/2020

THE ONLY ACCOMPLISHMENTS OF SOCIALISM ARE MASSIVE AMOUNTS OF DEATH, INCREASED POVERTY, DRASTICALLY LOWER STANDARDS OF LIVING, AND EXTREME GOVERNMENT CONTROL

THE ONLY ACCOMPLISHMENTS OF SOCIALISM ARE MASSIVE AMOUNTS OF DEATH, INCREASED POVERTY, DRASTICALLY LOWER STANDARDS OF LIVING, AND EXTREME GOVERNMENT CONTROL

THE ONLY ACCOMPLISHMENTS OF SOCIALISM ARE MASSIVE AMOUNTS OF DEATH, INCREASED POVERTY, DRASTICALLY LOWER STANDARDS OF LIVING, AND EXTREME GOVERNMENT CONTROL

THE ONLY ACCOMPLISHMENTS
OF SOCIALISM ARE MASSIVE
AMOUNTS OF DEATH,
INCREASED POVERTY,
DRASTICALLY LOWER
STANDARDS OF LIVING, AND
EXTREME GOVERNMENT
CONTROL

THE ONLY ACCOMPLISHMENTS
OF SOCIALISM ARE MASSIVE
AMOUNTS OF DEATH,
INCREASED POVERTY,
DRASTICALLY LOWER
STANDARDS OF LIVING, AND
EXTREME GOVERNMENT
CONTROL

THE ONLY ACCOMPLISHMENTS
OF SOCIALISM ARE MASSIVE
AMOUNTS OF DEATH,
INCREASED POVERTY,
DRASTICALLY LOWER
STANDARDS OF LIVING, AND
EXTREME GOVERNMENT
CONTROL

THE ONLY ACCOMPLISHMENTS OF SOCIALISM ARE MASSIVE AMOUNTS OF DEATH, INCREASED POVERTY, DRASTICALLY LOWER STANDARDS OF LIVING, AND EXTREME GOVERNMENT CONTROL

THE ONLY ACCOMPLISHMENTS OF SOCIALISM ARE MASSIVE AMOUNTS OF DEATH, INCREASED POVERTY, DRASTICALLY LOWER STANDARDS OF LIVING, AND EXTREME GOVERNMENT CONTROL

THE ONLY ACCOMPLISHMENTS OF SOCIALISM ARE MASSIVE AMOUNTS OF DEATH, INCREASED POVERTY, DRASTICALLY LOWER STANDARDS OF LIVING, AND EXTREME GOVERNMENT CONTROL

THE ONLY ACCOMPLISHMENTS OF SOCIALISM ARE MASSIVE AMOUNTS OF DEATH, INCREASED POVERTY, DRASTICALLY LOWER STANDARDS OF LIVING, AND EXTREME GOVERNMENT CONTROL

THE ONLY ACCOMPLISHMENTS
OF SOCIALISM ARE MASSIVE
AMOUNTS OF DEATH,
INCREASED POVERTY,
DRASTICALLY LOWER
STANDARDS OF LIVING, AND
EXTREME GOVERNMENT
CONTROL

THE ONLY ACCOMPLISHMENTS
OF SOCIALISM ARE MASSIVE
AMOUNTS OF DEATH,
INCREASED POVERTY,
DRASTICALLY LOWER
STANDARDS OF LIVING, AND
EXTREME GOVERNMENT
CONTROL

THE ONLY ACCOMPLISHMENTS OF SOCIALISM ARE MASSIVE AMOUNTS OF DEATH, INCREASED POVERTY, DRASTICALLY LOWER STANDARDS OF LIVING, AND EXTREME GOVERNMENT CONTROL

THE ONLY ACCOMPLISHMENTS
OF SOCIALISM ARE MASSIVE
AMOUNTS OF DEATH,
INCREASED POVERTY,
DRASTICALLY LOWER
STANDARDS OF LIVING, AND
EXTREME GOVERNMENT
CONTROL

THE ONLY ACCOMPLISHMENTS
OF SOCIALISM ARE MASSIVE
AMOUNTS OF DEATH,
INCREASED POVERTY,
DRASTICALLY LOWER
STANDARDS OF LIVING, AND
EXTREME GOVERNMENT
CONTROL

THE ONLY ACCOMPLISHMENTS OF SOCIALISM ARE MASSIVE AMOUNTS OF DEATH, INCREASED POVERTY, DRASTICALLY LOWER STANDARDS OF LIVING, AND EXTREME GOVERNMENT CONTROL

THE ONLY ACCOMPLISHMENTS
OF SOCIALISM ARE MASSIVE
AMOUNTS OF DEATH,
INCREASED POVERTY,
DRASTICALLY LOWER
STANDARDS OF LIVING, AND
EXTREME GOVERNMENT
CONTROL

THE ONLY ACCOMPLISHMENTS
OF SOCIALISM ARE MASSIVE
AMOUNTS OF DEATH,
INCREASED POVERTY,
DRASTICALLY LOWER
STANDARDS OF LIVING, AND
EXTREME GOVERNMENT
CONTROL

THE ONLY ACCOMPLISHMENTS
OF SOCIALISM ARE MASSIVE
AMOUNTS OF DEATH,
INCREASED POVERTY,
DRASTICALLY LOWER
STANDARDS OF LIVING, AND
EXTREME GOVERNMENT
CONTROL

THE ONLY ACCOMPLISHMENTS
OF SOCIALISM ARE MASSIVE
AMOUNTS OF DEATH,
INCREASED POVERTY,
DRASTICALLY LOWER
STANDARDS OF LIVING, AND
EXTREME GOVERNMENT
CONTROL

THE ONLY ACCOMPLISHMENTS OF SOCIALISM ARE MASSIVE AMOUNTS OF DEATH, INCREASED POVERTY, DRASTICALLY LOWER STANDARDS OF LIVING, AND EXTREME GOVERNMENT CONTROL

THE ONLY ACCOMPLISHMENTS
OF SOCIALISM ARE MASSIVE
AMOUNTS OF DEATH,
INCREASED POVERTY,
DRASTICALLY LOWER
STANDARDS OF LIVING, AND
EXTREME GOVERNMENT
CONTROL

THE ONLY ACCOMPLISHMENTS
OF SOCIALISM ARE MASSIVE
AMOUNTS OF DEATH,
INCREASED POVERTY,
DRASTICALLY LOWER
STANDARDS OF LIVING, AND
EXTREME GOVERNMENT
CONTROL

THE ONLY ACCOMPLISHMENTS
OF SOCIALISM ARE MASSIVE
AMOUNTS OF DEATH,
INCREASED POVERTY,
DRASTICALLY LOWER
STANDARDS OF LIVING, AND
EXTREME GOVERNMENT
CONTROL

THE ONLY ACCOMPLISHMENTS
OF SOCIALISM ARE MASSIVE
AMOUNTS OF DEATH,
INCREASED POVERTY,
DRASTICALLY LOWER
STANDARDS OF LIVING, AND
EXTREME GOVERNMENT
CONTROL

THE ONLY ACCOMPLISHMENTS
OF SOCIALISM ARE MASSIVE
AMOUNTS OF DEATH,
INCREASED POVERTY,
DRASTICALLY LOWER
STANDARDS OF LIVING, AND
EXTREME GOVERNMENT
CONTROL

THE ONLY ACCOMPLISHMENTS OF SOCIALISM ARE MASSIVE AMOUNTS OF DEATH, INCREASED POVERTY, DRASTICALLY LOWER STANDARDS OF LIVING, AND EXTREME GOVERNMENT CONTROL

THE ONLY ACCOMPLISHMENTS
OF SOCIALISM ARE MASSIVE
AMOUNTS OF DEATH,
INCREASED POVERTY,
DRASTICALLY LOWER
STANDARDS OF LIVING, AND
EXTREME GOVERNMENT
CONTROL

THE ONLY ACCOMPLISHMENTS
OF SOCIALISM ARE MASSIVE
AMOUNTS OF DEATH,
INCREASED POVERTY,
DRASTICALLY LOWER
STANDARDS OF LIVING, AND
EXTREME GOVERNMENT
CONTROL

THE ONLY ACCOMPLISHMENTS
OF SOCIALISM ARE MASSIVE
AMOUNTS OF DEATH,
INCREASED POVERTY,
DRASTICALLY LOWER
STANDARDS OF LIVING, AND
EXTREME GOVERNMENT
CONTROL

THE ONLY ACCOMPLISHMENTS
OF SOCIALISM ARE MASSIVE
AMOUNTS OF DEATH,
INCREASED POVERTY,
DRASTICALLY LOWER
STANDARDS OF LIVING, AND
EXTREME GOVERNMENT
CONTROL

THE ONLY ACCOMPLISHMENTS
OF SOCIALISM ARE MASSIVE
AMOUNTS OF DEATH,
INCREASED POVERTY,
DRASTICALLY LOWER
STANDARDS OF LIVING, AND
EXTREME GOVERNMENT
CONTROL

THE ONLY ACCOMPLISHMENTS
OF SOCIALISM ARE MASSIVE
AMOUNTS OF DEATH,
INCREASED POVERTY,
DRASTICALLY LOWER
STANDARDS OF LIVING, AND
EXTREME GOVERNMENT
CONTROL

THE ONLY ACCOMPLISHMENTS OF SOCIALISM ARE MASSIVE AMOUNTS OF DEATH, INCREASED POVERTY, DRASTICALLY LOWER STANDARDS OF LIVING, AND EXTREME GOVERNMENT CONTROL

THE ONLY ACCOMPLISHMENTS OF SOCIALISM ARE MASSIVE AMOUNTS OF DEATH, INCREASED POVERTY, DRASTICALLY LOWER STANDARDS OF LIVING, AND EXTREME GOVERNMENT CONTROL

THE ONLY ACCOMPLISHMENTS
OF SOCIALISM ARE MASSIVE
AMOUNTS OF DEATH,
INCREASED POVERTY,
DRASTICALLY LOWER
STANDARDS OF LIVING, AND
EXTREME GOVERNMENT
CONTROL

THE ONLY ACCOMPLISHMENTS OF SOCIALISM ARE MASSIVE AMOUNTS OF DEATH, INCREASED POVERTY, DRASTICALLY LOWER STANDARDS OF LIVING, AND EXTREME GOVERNMENT CONTROL

THE ONLY ACCOMPLISHMENTS
OF SOCIALISM ARE MASSIVE
AMOUNTS OF DEATH,
INCREASED POVERTY,
DRASTICALLY LOWER
STANDARDS OF LIVING, AND
EXTREME GOVERNMENT
CONTROL

THE ONLY ACCOMPLISHMENTS
OF SOCIALISM ARE MASSIVE
AMOUNTS OF DEATH,
INCREASED POVERTY,
DRASTICALLY LOWER
STANDARDS OF LIVING, AND
EXTREME GOVERNMENT
CONTROL

THE ONLY ACCOMPLISHMENTS
OF SOCIALISM ARE MASSIVE
AMOUNTS OF DEATH,
INCREASED POVERTY,
DRASTICALLY LOWER
STANDARDS OF LIVING, AND
EXTREME GOVERNMENT
CONTROL

THE ONLY ACCOMPLISHMENTS
OF SOCIALISM ARE MASSIVE
AMOUNTS OF DEATH,
INCREASED POVERTY,
DRASTICALLY LOWER
STANDARDS OF LIVING, AND
EXTREME GOVERNMENT
CONTROL

THE ONLY ACCOMPLISHMENTS OF SOCIALISM ARE MASSIVE AMOUNTS OF DEATH, INCREASED POVERTY, DRASTICALLY LOWER STANDARDS OF LIVING, AND EXTREME GOVERNMENT CONTROL

THE ONLY ACCOMPLISHMENTS OF SOCIALISM ARE MASSIVE AMOUNTS OF DEATH, INCREASED POVERTY, DRASTICALLY LOWER STANDARDS OF LIVING, AND EXTREME GOVERNMENT CONTROL

THE ONLY ACCOMPLISHMENTS
OF SOCIALISM ARE MASSIVE
AMOUNTS OF DEATH,
INCREASED POVERTY,
DRASTICALLY LOWER
STANDARDS OF LIVING, AND
EXTREME GOVERNMENT
CONTROL

THE ONLY ACCOMPLISHMENTS OF SOCIALISM ARE MASSIVE AMOUNTS OF DEATH, INCREASED POVERTY, DRASTICALLY LOWER STANDARDS OF LIVING, AND EXTREME GOVERNMENT CONTROL

THE ONLY ACCOMPLISHMENTS OF SOCIALISM ARE MASSIVE AMOUNTS OF DEATH, INCREASED POVERTY, DRASTICALLY LOWER STANDARDS OF LIVING, AND EXTREME GOVERNMENT CONTROL

THE ONLY ACCOMPLISHMENTS
OF SOCIALISM ARE MASSIVE
AMOUNTS OF DEATH,
INCREASED POVERTY,
DRASTICALLY LOWER
STANDARDS OF LIVING, AND
EXTREME GOVERNMENT
CONTROL

THE ONLY ACCOMPLISHMENTS
OF SOCIALISM ARE MASSIVE
AMOUNTS OF DEATH,
INCREASED POVERTY,
DRASTICALLY LOWER
STANDARDS OF LIVING, AND
EXTREME GOVERNMENT
CONTROL

THE ONLY ACCOMPLISHMENTS OF SOCIALISM ARE MASSIVE AMOUNTS OF DEATH, INCREASED POVERTY, DRASTICALLY LOWER STANDARDS OF LIVING, AND EXTREME GOVERNMENT CONTROL

THE ONLY ACCOMPLISHMENTS OF SOCIALISM ARE MASSIVE AMOUNTS OF DEATH, INCREASED POVERTY, DRASTICALLY LOWER STANDARDS OF LIVING, AND EXTREME GOVERNMENT CONTROL

THE ONLY ACCOMPLISHMENTS
OF SOCIALISM ARE MASSIVE
AMOUNTS OF DEATH,
INCREASED POVERTY,
DRASTICALLY LOWER
STANDARDS OF LIVING, AND
EXTREME GOVERNMENT
CONTROL

THE ONLY ACCOMPLISHMENTS
OF SOCIALISM ARE MASSIVE
AMOUNTS OF DEATH,
INCREASED POVERTY,
DRASTICALLY LOWER
STANDARDS OF LIVING, AND
EXTREME GOVERNMENT
CONTROL

THE ONLY ACCOMPLISHMENTS
OF SOCIALISM ARE MASSIVE
AMOUNTS OF DEATH,
INCREASED POVERTY,
DRASTICALLY LOWER
STANDARDS OF LIVING, AND
EXTREME GOVERNMENT
CONTROL

THE ONLY ACCOMPLISHMENTS
OF SOCIALISM ARE MASSIVE
AMOUNTS OF DEATH,
INCREASED POVERTY,
DRASTICALLY LOWER
STANDARDS OF LIVING, AND
EXTREME GOVERNMENT
CONTROL

THE ONLY ACCOMPLISHMENTS
OF SOCIALISM ARE MASSIVE
AMOUNTS OF DEATH,
INCREASED POVERTY,
DRASTICALLY LOWER
STANDARDS OF LIVING, AND
EXTREME GOVERNMENT
CONTROL

THE ONLY ACCOMPLISHMENTS OF SOCIALISM ARE MASSIVE AMOUNTS OF DEATH, INCREASED POVERTY, DRASTICALLY LOWER STANDARDS OF LIVING, AND EXTREME GOVERNMENT CONTROL

THE ONLY ACCOMPLISHMENTS
OF SOCIALISM ARE MASSIVE
AMOUNTS OF DEATH,
INCREASED POVERTY,
DRASTICALLY LOWER
STANDARDS OF LIVING, AND
EXTREME GOVERNMENT
CONTROL

THE ONLY ACCOMPLISHMENTS
OF SOCIALISM ARE MASSIVE
AMOUNTS OF DEATH,
INCREASED POVERTY,
DRASTICALLY LOWER
STANDARDS OF LIVING, AND
EXTREME GOVERNMENT
CONTROL

THE ONLY ACCOMPLISHMENTS OF SOCIALISM ARE MASSIVE AMOUNTS OF DEATH, INCREASED POVERTY, DRASTICALLY LOWER STANDARDS OF LIVING, AND EXTREME GOVERNMENT CONTROL

THE ONLY ACCOMPLISHMENTS OF SOCIALISM ARE MASSIVE AMOUNTS OF DEATH, INCREASED POVERTY, DRASTICALLY LOWER STANDARDS OF LIVING, AND EXTREME GOVERNMENT CONTROL

THE ONLY ACCOMPLISHMENTS OF SOCIALISM ARE MASSIVE AMOUNTS OF DEATH, INCREASED POVERTY, DRASTICALLY LOWER STANDARDS OF LIVING, AND EXTREME GOVERNMENT CONTROL

THE ONLY ACCOMPLISHMENTS
OF SOCIALISM ARE MASSIVE
AMOUNTS OF DEATH,
INCREASED POVERTY,
DRASTICALLY LOWER
STANDARDS OF LIVING, AND
EXTREME GOVERNMENT
CONTROL

THE ONLY ACCOMPLISHMENTS OF SOCIALISM ARE MASSIVE AMOUNTS OF DEATH, INCREASED POVERTY, DRASTICALLY LOWER STANDARDS OF LIVING, AND EXTREME GOVERNMENT CONTROL

THE ONLY ACCOMPLISHMENTS
OF SOCIALISM ARE MASSIVE
AMOUNTS OF DEATH,
INCREASED POVERTY,
DRASTICALLY LOWER
STANDARDS OF LIVING, AND
EXTREME GOVERNMENT
CONTROL

THE ONLY ACCOMPLISHMENTS OF SOCIALISM ARE MASSIVE AMOUNTS OF DEATH, INCREASED POVERTY, DRASTICALLY LOWER STANDARDS OF LIVING, AND EXTREME GOVERNMENT CONTROL

THE ONLY ACCOMPLISHMENTS OF SOCIALISM ARE MASSIVE AMOUNTS OF DEATH, INCREASED POVERTY, DRASTICALLY LOWER STANDARDS OF LIVING, AND EXTREME GOVERNMENT CONTROL

THE ONLY ACCOMPLISHMENTS
OF SOCIALISM ARE MASSIVE
AMOUNTS OF DEATH,
INCREASED POVERTY,
DRASTICALLY LOWER
STANDARDS OF LIVING, AND
EXTREME GOVERNMENT
CONTROL

THE ONLY ACCOMPLISHMENTS OF SOCIALISM ARE MASSIVE AMOUNTS OF DEATH, INCREASED POVERTY, DRASTICALLY LOWER STANDARDS OF LIVING, AND EXTREME GOVERNMENT CONTROL

THE ONLY ACCOMPLISHMENTS OF SOCIALISM ARE MASSIVE AMOUNTS OF DEATH, INCREASED POVERTY, DRASTICALLY LOWER STANDARDS OF LIVING, AND EXTREME GOVERNMENT CONTROL

THE ONLY ACCOMPLISHMENTS
OF SOCIALISM ARE MASSIVE
AMOUNTS OF DEATH,
INCREASED POVERTY,
DRASTICALLY LOWER
STANDARDS OF LIVING, AND
EXTREME GOVERNMENT
CONTROL

THE ONLY ACCOMPLISHMENTS
OF SOCIALISM ARE MASSIVE
AMOUNTS OF DEATH,
INCREASED POVERTY,
DRASTICALLY LOWER
STANDARDS OF LIVING, AND
EXTREME GOVERNMENT
CONTROL

THE ONLY ACCOMPLISHMENTS
OF SOCIALISM ARE MASSIVE
AMOUNTS OF DEATH,
INCREASED POVERTY,
DRASTICALLY LOWER
STANDARDS OF LIVING, AND
EXTREME GOVERNMENT
CONTROL

THE ONLY ACCOMPLISHMENTS
OF SOCIALISM ARE MASSIVE
AMOUNTS OF DEATH,
INCREASED POVERTY,
DRASTICALLY LOWER
STANDARDS OF LIVING, AND
EXTREME GOVERNMENT
CONTROL

THE ONLY ACCOMPLISHMENTS
OF SOCIALISM ARE MASSIVE
AMOUNTS OF DEATH,
INCREASED POVERTY,
DRASTICALLY LOWER
STANDARDS OF LIVING, AND
EXTREME GOVERNMENT
CONTROL

THE ONLY ACCOMPLISHMENTS OF SOCIALISM ARE MASSIVE AMOUNTS OF DEATH, INCREASED POVERTY, DRASTICALLY LOWER STANDARDS OF LIVING, AND EXTREME GOVERNMENT CONTROL

Seriously, Socialism has failed every single time in every single place it has been implemented. Previous examples of Socialistic "success" by Socialist advocates, such as several Nordic states, have never been valid points in favor of Socialism because not only have the governments of many of those countries now collapsed due to economic turmoil within recent years of this book's publishing, those countries were never true Socialist countries- they were extremely heavily regulated Capitalist

countries. Truly, Socialism has

always only led to massive amounts

of death, increased poverty,

drastically lower standards of living,

and extreme government control.

About the Author

James King is a 2019 graduate from Truett McConnell University, a Southern Baptist college in North Georgia, where he earned a degree in the Great Commission (Evangelism). In addition to *Making the Case for Socialism*, James has written *Visions of Yonah* (a historical picture book of White County, Georgia), *The Elephant in the Sanctuary: Comparing the Republican Platform to the Bible*, and *Faces in these Hills* (a book of local ghost stories from White County, Georgia). All four books are available for purchase on Amazon in both paperback and Kindle formats. Currently, James serves as the Minister of Music for a Baptist Church in Toccoa, Georgia, is the Chairman of Young Republicans of Northeast Georgia, cheers on the University of Georgia Bulldogs every Fall, is committed to Making America Great Again, and married the love of his life on August 1, 2020!

www.ingramcontent.com/pod-product-compliance
Lightning Source LLC
Chambersburg PA
CBHW031923270726

48655CB00011BA/2522